MW00834185

GALE
CENGAGE Learning

Novels for Students, Volume 35

Project Editor: Sara Constantakis Rights Acquisition and Management: Margaret Chamberlain-Gaston, Leitha Etheridge-Sims, Kelly Quin, Aja Perales Composition: Evi Abou-El-Seoud Manufacturing: Drew Kalasky

Imaging: John Watkins

Product Design: Pamela A. E. Galbreath, Jennifer Wahi Content Conversion: Katrina Coach Product Manager: Meggin Condino

For product information and technology assistance, contact us at **Gale Customer Support, 1-800-877-4253.**

For permission to use material from this text or product, submit all requests online at **www.cengage.com/permissions**.

Further permissions questions can be emailed to **permissionrequest@cengage.com** While every effort has been made to ensure the reliability of the information presented in this publication, Gale, a part of Cengage Learning, does not guarantee the accuracy of the data contained herein. Gale accepts no payment for listing; and inclusion in the publication of any organization, agency, institution, publication, service, or individual does not imply endorsement of the editors or publisher. Errors brought to the attention of the publisher and verified to the satisfaction of the publisher will be corrected in future editions.

Gale
27500 Drake Rd.
Farmington Hills, MI, 48331-3535

ISBN-13: 978-1-4144-6698-9
ISBN-10: 1-4144-6698-6
ISSN 1094-3552

This title is also available as an e-book.
ISBN-13: 978-1-4144-7364-2

ISBN-10: 1-4144-7364-8
Contact your Gale, a part of Cengage Learning sales
representative for ordering information.

Printed in the United States of America
1 2 3 4 5 6 7 14 13 12 11 10

April Morning

Howard Fast

1961

Introduction

Howard Fast's young-adult novel *April Morning* is more than a story of war. It is the story of a fifteen-year-old boy finding himself and becoming an adult in the middle of a revolution. When the story begins, Adam Cooper is a typical teen, living in eighteenth-century rural Massachusetts. As he does his morning chores, he grumbles about his parents not taking him seriously and treating him as if he were still a child, but everything in Adam's life is about to change. In just a little over twenty four hours, he will be looked upon as a man—a successful soldier who is consider ed mature enough to marry and to become the new head of his family's household.

Fast is well known for taking stories from history books and turning them into gripping tales as seen through the eyes of common folk. Rather than narrating this novel, for example, through the experience of the high-ranking officers whose names appear frequently in the historical accounts, Fast creates a fictional character who witnesses all the same events but from a different and more personal point of view. In this novel, readers feel both the pride and the fear of the teenage protagonist who wants to be respected as an adult. Then, when he is suddenly given the chance, he questions why he wanted to grow up so fast.

April Morning was published in 1961, a transitional period for young-adult novels, which were finally coming into their own. Authors of stories written for teens were developing more serious subjects and were writing in a more literary form than had been used for young-adult books in previous decades. Fast's *April Morning* was considered one of the first to take on these new elements. J. Donald Adams, writing a review for the *New York Times*, predicted back in the 1960s that this novel would "some day reach the standing of an American classic."

Author Biography

Fast was born in New York City on November 11, 1914. His father held various positions as a manual laborer. Because his father earned only a meager wage, when Fast was twelve, he sold newspapers to provide more income for the family. After graduating from high school, Fast left home and traveled across the country by hopping free rides on railroad cars, mingling with train hobos along the way. It was during this time that Fast wrote his first novel, a historical romance called *Two Valleys* (1933), which enjoyed moderate success. His second book, *Conceived in Liberty, A Novel of Valley Forge* (1939), brought him more fame as well as more money. It was with his second novel that Fast developed an interest in the American Revolution, a theme he would continue to pursue in his 1961 novel *April Morning*.

As his career as a writer progressed, Fast soon discovered his love of retelling history. For example, his 1941 novel *The Last Frontier* tells the litle known story of a Cheyenne uprising that took place in 1878, and his best-selling 1944 novel *Freedom Road* relates the story of the Reconstruction Era after the Civil War from the experience of a former slave. In another popular novel, *Citizen Tom Paine* (1943), Fast recounts the life of the man who spoke for the common man as Paine urged the colonies to go to war against Britain in the American Revolutionary War.

Fast became embroiled in politics in the 1950s. He had joined the Communist Party and was subpoenaed by the U.S. Congress to appear before the House Un-American Activities Committee. While facing the committee, Fast was asked to name his fellow members in the U.S. Communist Party. However, Fast refused and for this was sent to prison. This did not stop him from writing, though. While in jail, Fast produced one of his more famous novels, *Spartacus* (1951), which nine years later was adapted to film. However, once word spread that Fast was a communist, his books were taken off library shelves, and publishers were not as enthusiastic about publishing his new works, so he chose a pen name, E. V. Cunningham. Under this name, he wrote detective stories, such as *Sylvia* (1960) and *Alice* (1963). It was during this time that Fast moved to Los Angeles, California. He continued writing novels but also wrote plays and scripts. In 1975, an Emmy Award for outstanding writing in a drama series for his television script "The Ambassadors" (1963), which was part of the series *Benjamin Franklin*.

Fast produced more than eighty novels before his death on March 12, 2003, at the age of eighty-eight. He had returned to the East Coast in 1980 and lived in Connecticut with his wife, Bette, until she died in 1994. Fast was survived by his second wife, Mercedes, his daughter, Rachel, his son, Jonathan, and several stepchildren and grandchildren.

The Afternoon

April Morning opens on the afternoon of April 18, 1775, in the town of Lexington, Massachusetts. Adam Cooper, the fifteen-year-old protagonist, is doing chores while grumbling about how his father, Moses, under-appreciates him. Moses appears to be a stern father who does not waste his words but is quick to throw out a proverb, such as "slow to start and quick to finish," in his appraisal of his son's work ethics. When Moses tells Adam to draw water from their well, the boy recites the words of a spell. His eleven-year-old brother, Levi, overhears this and tells their father. Later that night at the dinner table, Moses reprimands Adam. First, he states that although Adam is tall enough to be a man he is not acting like a man. This is exactly what has been bothering Adam lately. He senses that he is approaching manhood, but no matter what he does, his father will not acknowledge that Adam is growing beyond childhood. Repeating the spell over the water is something Moses has declared superstitious and thus childish.

Granny Cooper, Moses's mother and Adam and Levi's grandmother, chastises her son for making a big fuss about Adam's reciting the spell. Though Adam's grandmother sometimes reprimands him for talking too freely about controversial topics, she enjoys Adam's conversations and often stands up for him. Granny Cooper also has a tendency to continue to speak to her son, Moses, as if he were still a child.

Media Adaptations

- Delbert Mann directed the film version of *April Morning*, starring Tommy Lee Jones as Moses Cooper and Chad Lowe as Adam. The film was released in 1988 and was shown on television by Hallmark Hall of Fame Productions.

- Recorded Books offers a 1988 audio presentation of Fast's *April Morning* in both CD and audio cassette forms. Jamie Hanes is the reader.

Joseph Simmons, Adam's cousin, comes to talk

to Moses about a speech he has been asked to make on the universal rights of men. Joseph and Moses are going to an important committee meeting after dinner. Adam asks if he can also attend. Moses again challenges Adam, questioning whether he is ready to be a man. He tells Adam that the proof of manhood is found in his "will to work and the ability to use his mind and his judgment." Adam backs down, concerned that he does not yet have such proof. After his father leaves, Adam asks his mother and grandmother why his father disapproves of him. His father always finds fault with him, Adam tells them. They answer that is just the way Moses is. Granny Cooper adds that Moses finds fault with everyone.

The Evening

Adam overhears his father talking to his mother about what happened at the meeting. Moses dislikes the committee's attention on weaponry, preferring arbitration. Adam says his father "deeply believed that if you could win an argument, you could win a war."

Adam visits Ruth Simmons, with whom he has been friends for most of his life. Ruth appears to have her mind set on eventually marrying Adam. However, Adam is not quite prepared to even think that far into the future. He notices, though, that Ruth is changing—she is turning into a woman. When Adam talks about possibly joining his Uncle Ishmael and sailing to the Indies, Ruth says that would make her very lonely. It pleases Adam that Ruth would miss him.

When Adam returns home, he finds Levi cleaning Adam's gun. Though he is still angry with Levi for telling their father about the water spell, Adam eventually softens and thanks Levi for the good job he has done. Levi has fantasies about being a soldier. He and his friends play games that entail killing imaginary redcoats.

After Adam goes to bed, he overhears his parents. His mother suggests that Moses find some way to show Adam that he loves him. At first, Moses rebels against this idea, stating that he is raising his son in the same way his father raised him. However, Moses relents and says he will think the matter over.

The Night

In the middle of the night, Levi runs to Adam to tell him about a nightmare he had about his own death. Adam takes Levi to the window and tries to calm him down. While standing there, Levi hears horse hooves beating against the road, an unusual occurrence in the middle of the night. Moses comes into the room and the boys tell him what they have heard. They also heard someone shouting. Moses is concerned. He suspects it is a messenger from Cambridge, Massachusetts, and he leaves the house to find out what is happening. Adam follows his father. A crowd has gathered around the rider, who tells them that a large troop of British soldiers is marching toward Lexington. Their destination is Concord, where they plan to destroy military supplies.

Jonas Parker wants to immediately call up the militia. Some people, including Sam Hodley, do not believe the British Army is really coming. The Reverend asks how they could fight this army, if it really is coming. Lexington has, at most, only seventy or eighty men who could fight, whereas the British might number nearly a thousand. Opposing the Reverend is Moses, who is against fighting but who is also an intellectual who likes to argue with the Reverend. Moses gives one of his rousing speeches, and by the time he stops talking, he has convinced the people that it is their moral obligation to stand up to the British and fight for their rights. Adam is proud of his father's speech and follows the men to sign the muster book, a form of enlisting in the military. When Cousin Simmons sees Adam, he says to him: "A boy went to bed and a man awakened."

When Adam returns home, he overhears his mother telling Moses she is angry that he allowed Adam to sign up. "He's just a boy," Sarah says. Then Moses says, "Yesterday, he was a boy. ... Tonight, he's not."

The Morning

Later, as Moses and Adam return to the village center, Moses puts his arm around his son's shoulders. This is the first sign of affection that

Adam can remember receiving from his father. Moses then says: "I have found that when adversity confronts them, the Cooper men stand firmly." This is Moses's way of telling Adam that he has proven that he is now a man.

When they arrive at the common, a group of men is there with their guns. The coming of the British Army has been confirmed. However, the Reverend and Moses recommend that the men not be too eager to shoot. They hope the British are willing to negotiate. If the British refuse to talk, the Lexington men should let the British pass by. The British outnumber them, so there is no way of stopping them. When shots are heard in the distance, the men grow silent. Moses, Jonas Parker, and the Reverend stand at the front. The road is filled with redcoats—British soldiers—"so that they appeared to be an endless force and an endless number."

The British major, Pitcairn, commands his troops to line up opposite the Lexington militia. At this point, Adam says: "I realized, and I believed that everyone else a round me realized, that this was not to be an exercise or a parade or an argument, but something undreamed of and unimagined." The Reverend attempts to speak to Major Pitcairn, but he does not listen and instead orders the Lexington men to put down their weapons.

The younger men want to comply, but Jonas Parker tells them to hold their positions. Then a shot is heard. Immediately afterward, a British soldier aims his gun at Moses. Adam sees his father fall.

Filled with fear, Adam runs. As he does, he sees men lying on the ground, wounded or dead. Samuel Hodley has a hole in his neck. Jonas Parker is bleeding from his belly. Adam sees a British soldier run a bayonet through Parker's back. When he comes to a storage hut, Adam crawls in and hides. While he sits there shaking, Adam reexamines what he has just been through. It is then that the death of his father finally hits him. His father "would never come home again," Adam tells himself.

The Forenoon

Moses hides in the shed until he thinks the British soldiers have left. He sneaks out and runs for a meadow. He runs fast and hard, barely noticing what is up ahead of him. When he reaches a stone wall, he collapses on it and into a pair of strong arms. He fights to get free but is stopped by Solomon Chandler, who is part of the Massachusetts militia. Chandler makes Adam turn around to see the two soldiers he was running from and who are standing on the other side of the field. They are no longer chasing him.

Chandler, an older man, shares his lunch with Adam and gives him insights about the British soldiers. Adam tells Chandler about the events in Lexington, and Chandler commiserates with Adam's sadness over the loss of his father. Adam confesses he feels he acted cowardly in running away. However, Chandler tells him that is exactly the proper tactic in dealing with the British. The colonists cannot defeat the British by using the same military tactics as the redcoats. The colonists will inflict the most damage by continually shooting at the British and then running away.

Chandler thinks the Concord militia will meet the British at North Bridge. The militia's plan is not to stop the British as the Lexington men had tried but rather to kill as many as they can, shooting at them from the sides of the road. When they reach a meeting place, Asley's Pasture, Adam is reunited with Cousin Simmons and the Reverend, whom Adam had worried might have been killed in Lexington.

The Midday

As men gather from the surrounding towns, Adam learns there are several meeting points along the main road where committee members have gathered. One of the bigger groups is poised at North Bridge, outside Concord. Adam, upon hearing this information, is proud of his father and his role in organizing the communities in eastern Massachusetts, in preparation for them to confront the British.

As the men wait for the British to turn around at Concord and march back to Boston, Cousin Simmons talks to Adam about Moses's death. Simmons insinuates there is a chance that he might die in the war and asks Adam to look after his family, especially his daughter Ruth. As Simmons is talking, they hear gunshots in the distance.

Chandler tells everyone to break up into small groups along the sides of the road. They should hide themselves as best they can, shoot, and then run quickly out of the reach of the British gunshots. Adam is with Cousin Simmons and the Reverend. Chandler tells Adam not to shoot his gun until he can count the buttons on the British soldiers' coats; his gun can have an effect only at very close range. When Chandler says they are fighting "in God's cause," the Reverend disputes this point: "Isn't it enough to kill in freedom's name? No one kills in God's cause. He can only ask God's forgiveness."

As the British soldiers approach, Adam notices how many are wounded. Blood is everywhere on their uniforms. They looked tired, angry, and full of fear. After Adam takes his first shot, he freezes in the spot. Cousin Simmons saves him by grabbing Adam by the arm and pulling him away. Later, as the fighting continues, Cousin Simmons explains to Adam that though he does not believe in fighting or war, their actions are now necessary because they are fighting for their freedom and their land. On the other hand, Simmons tells Adam that Chandler fights out of revenge. Adam observes some of the men around him, including Chandler. He hears them boasting of how many British they have killed. Adam is disgusted with their talk. He has seen young boys his own age mortally wounded. He saw a soldier's head blown off. He has had enough of the war.

The Afternoon

Adam is ready to forget all about fighting, but Cousin Simmons tells him this is just the beginning. The war could last years. Chandler confirms this as he rallies the men to follow him to where they can ambush the British. Chandler wants to clear the British out of their towns.

Adam is so worn out that he falls asleep in the middle of a battle. While he sleeps, Cousin Simmons and the Reverend look for him, praying that Adam has not been killed. As they search, they mention how proud they are of him. As they approach the place where Adam has fallen asleep, Adam hears their conversation, which makes him feel good. When Simmons and the Reverend find him, they greet him almost as if he were their own son, they are so pleased that Adam is alive. Cousin Simmons tells Adam it is time to go home. The British have been driven away from Lexington. New committeemen have taken over the pursuit.

Near his home, Adam is greeted by his brother. Levi had heard that Adam was dead and can hardly believe that he is actually alive. When Adam enters his home, he finds his mother and grandmother are surrounded by neighbor women, who are there to prepare for Moses's funeral. Adam is led to his father's room to pay his respects. Adam is too numb from all the death he has seen that day to mourn for his father. He will remember him later, he states, not as a corpse but as he had lived. Adam returns downstairs and talks to Levi. He makes his younger brother realize that the two of them must now take on their father's responsibilities. They must take care of their mother. Levi tells Adam about the British soldiers that stormed their town while Adam was away, stealing food and crops, burning houses, and taking away horses and wagons. Then Adam's mother comes to him. She is crying and has no idea how they are going to survive without Moses. Adam attempts to soothe her, telling her everything will work out. Cousin Simmons then arrives and, with several other men, carries Moses's casket to the meetinghouse.

The Evening

Ruth accompanies Adam as he takes candles to the meetinghouse. His mother wants to make sure Moses's body will not be left in the dark. As Adam bemoans his surprisingly quick passage from childhood to manhood, he looks at Ruth and realizes she looks different to him, more beautiful than ever before. Ruth wraps her arms around him and kisses him. She tells him that when she heard the news that he was dead, everything died within her. She tells him she loves him and is not ashamed of saying so. Adam feels the same. He realizes there could not be another woman for him. Ruth knows so much about him and accepts him for who he is. It would take forever for another woman to learn as much about him.

Ruth asks whether Adam killed anyone. Adam does not think so; he says he did not hate anyone enough to kill him. When Ruth asks whether the British will return, Adam says no. Nothing will ever be the same. The Americans have now committed to fighting the British so they can gain their freedom.

They will become better at fighting the British, Adam tells her.

The Reverend sees them and tells Adam that the Committeemen have called a muster. Ruth does not want Adam to sign it. Adam says he has not made up his mind yet, but when Adam goes home, his grandmother knows better. She tells Adam that sooner or later he will once again leave. Adam tries to deny this but cannot. When he goes to bed, he gives thanks that the day is finally over. Before falling asleep, he says farewell to his childhood.

Solomon Chandler

Adam meets Solomon Chandler when Adam is running away from the British soldiers. Adam describes Chandler as a skinny but strong man, with a long face and yellow teeth. At first, Adam admires Solomon's strength, wisdom about war, and generosity. However, after hanging around him for several hours during that day of war, Adam comes to resent Solomon. Adam believes that Solomon, who has fought in many wars, enjoys killing.

Adam Cooper

Adam is the fifteen-year-old protagonist of this novel. The story is told from his perspective. Though he is considered a boy in the first section of this book, as he witnesses war, sees his father die, and shoots at British soldiers, he is quickly accepted as a man.

Manhood comes to Adam at a high cost. He is terrorized by the killing and brutality that he witnesses, especially the murder of his father. Though the experiences of the war force him into maturity, becoming a man is not as much fun as he once thought it might be. He must take on the responsibilities at home. He must watch over his mother, his grandmother, and his brother, Levi. He also contemplates marriage to Ruth, something he had thought would not occur for a long time into the future. The war has changed him, though. He must say good-bye to his childhood, for there is no turning back.

According to Cousin Simmons and the Reverend, as well Solomon Chandler, Adam has matured in a very honorable way. He has handled himself well in the midst of battle. He has not complained about the lack of sleep, the fear that nearly overwhelmed him, or any of the challenges that he has been forced to face. Though he is saddened by the loss of his father, he has not been distracted by his sorrow.

Granny Cooper

Granny Cooper, the mother of Moses Cooper, is a widow whose other children all died before the start of the novel. Granny lives with Moses, his wife, and their two children. Though her relationship with Levi is never portrayed, she is obviously close to Adam. She enjoys his company. Though Adam sometimes shocks her with some of his radical thoughts, she appreciates that he thinks deeply about things. Granny often sticks up for Adam when Moses reprimands, disagrees with, or criticizes him. Granny is not afraid to speak up to her son, though she is living in his house and is the head of the household. She often talks to Moses as if he were still her juvenile son.

Levi Cooper

Levi is Adam's eleven-year-old brother, the son of Moses and Sarah. The author uses Levi to compare the boy's rather immature thoughts about war with Adam's real experience with death on the battlefield.

Levi lives in a fantasy world; he believes war might be fun. Though Levi gets Adam in trouble by reporting that he recited a spell, it is obvious that the young boy admires and loves his older brother. It is through Levi that Adam can see how much he has changed. When Adam returns home after the battle with the British soldiers, he understands so much more about life and war than Levi can comprehend. Levi still lives in his fantasies of the adult world, whereas Adam has witnessed the realities of war and the challenges of growing up.

Moses Cooper

Moses is Adam and Levi's father, Granny Cooper's son, and Sarah Cooper's husband. As captain of the Lexington Committee and with his flair for elegant rhetoric, Moses is viewed as one of the most prominent men of Lexington. People look up to him, and they are often roused by his eloquent and rational judgments. Although he is very capable in the public realm, Moses is not always quite as eloquent at home. He can be very critical of Adam, which makes Moses appear harsh and cold-hearted.

Moses insists that he does not want to go to

war with the British, but when British soldiers march into Lexington, Moses wants them to know that he does not approve of their presence. He wants to demand his right to freedom from British rule. Moses is the first of the Lexington men who are shot down. However, before he dies, Moses confesses to Adam how proud he is of him for stepping up and taking on the responsibility of defending their town. Moses finally acknowledges that Adam has become a man.

Sarah Cooper

Sarah is Adam and Levi's mother and Moses's wife. She is the peacemaker at home, especially between Moses and Adam. She is a good cook and supportive mother. Her character as an independent person, however, is not very well developed. Sarah is shown mostly in a supportive role, attending to the men in her family. When Moses is killed, Sarah leans on Adam, whom she is hoping will step up to the task of taking on many of the duties for which his father was once responsible.

Joshua Dover

Joshua is Adam's cousin. Along with Solomon Chandler, he helps to organize the committeemen and the militia as they gather in the fields after the killing in Lexington. Cousin Dover, as Adam calls him, attempts to keep a record of the events of every battle as they happen.

Samuel Hodley

Samuel was one of the Lexington villagers who did not believe the British were coming. Adam sees Samuel mortally wounded with a hole in his neck after the British march through his town.

Grandfather Isaac

Isaac, a sea captain, was Sarah Cooper's grandfather. He was a topic of gossip in the family because he had two wives. He kept them separate, with one living in Boston and the other in Philadelphia. His Philadelphia wife was part Shawnee. When Isaac died, he left Sarah a large amount of money, which Moses believed absolved the grandfather from all the wrong doings he had done during his lifetime.

Ishmael Jamison

Ishmael Jamison is Adam's uncle on his mother's side. He is a ship captain and had wanted Adam to join him for a voyage to the Indies. Ruth refers to Ishmael as a smuggler. Adam defends his uncle, blaming the British for taking away his uncle's legal trade. His uncle, Adam proclaims, is merely making a living as best he can.

Jonas Parker

Jonas was elected captain of the Lexington militia. Moses Cooper often argues with Jonas about who is the top commander of the town. Moses is the head of the committee and believes in arbitration. Jonas, as head of the militia, believes in using force, if necessary, against the British. Adam sees a British soldier push a bayonet through Jonas, which makes Adam realize he must run for his life.

Isaiah Peterkin

Isaiah is a deacon in the Lexington church. Adam refers to Isaiah as being "mean and wicked and two-faced." Granny Cooper chastises Adam for calling Isaiah names. However, Adam states that he is merely telling a truth that everyone else already knows.

Major Pitcairn

Major Pitcairn is the head of the British forces that march through Lexington. He is unwilling to negotiate with the Lexington men and nearly runs down the Reverend and Moses with his horse when they try to talk to him.

The Reverend

The Reverend is the religious leader and second best debater in Lexington. He and Moses often argue over political and religious issues. After Moses is killed, the Reverend looks after Adam as if he were his own son. He also helps Adam work through his emotions of having lost his father.

Rider

An unnamed rider arrives in the middle of the night with news of the British troops heading for Lexington. Though he is not identified in this novel, there is a good chance that the author modeled him on Paul Revere, who rode through the night to warn the colonists of the British Army's approach.

Joseph Simmons

Joseph is described as a big man who loves food. Joseph is Adam's cousin and Ruth's father and lives close to the Cooper house. He is a blacksmith. Joseph's five brothers had shared a financial interest in a slave ship because this was extremely profitable. This caused Joseph to break away from his brothers and never speak to them again.

Cousin Simmons, as Adam refers to him, watches over Adam after Moses dies. He feels responsible for Adam's safety. However, before he and Adam face a second encounter with the British soldiers, Cousin Simmons fears for his own life. He asks Adam, if something should happen to him, to look after his family, especially his daughter Ruth.

Rebecca Simmons

Rebecca is Joseph Simmons's wife and Ruth's mother. Rebecca plays a very minor role in this story, merely holding the position of mother and wife with very little to say. She offers Adam some pie when he comes to visit Ruth. She is also at

Adam's house, helping Adam's mother with the funeral of Moses.

Ruth Simmons

Ruth is Adam's second cousin and Joseph Simmons's daughter. She is three months younger than Adam and is strong willed but has a sympathetic heart. Adam likes talking to her, pressing his new ideas on her and relying on her to help him sort his thoughts. It is obvious that Ruth likes Adam, as she is the one who initiates the few kisses that they share. However, after Adam comes home from the battles with the British, Ruth tells Adam that she loves him. Ruth is the only woman Adam can imagine marrying.

Susan Simmons

Susan Simmons is the widowed sister of Rebecca Simmons. Susan lives with Rebecca and her family. Once when Adam comes to the Simmons's house looking for Ruth, Susan asks Adam to read a passage from the Bible.

Coming of Age

April Morning begins with the fifteen-year-old protagonist, Adam, wishing that his parents would take him seriously. He is tired of being treated like a child. He wants his father, in particular, to see him as a man, but his father refuses. Thus, Fast sets up a major theme in his story: Adam's coming of age. A novel with a coming-of-age theme usually presents a young teen, male or female, who is on the cusp of becoming an adult. The protagonist finds himself or herself caught between the two worlds of childhood and adulthood. In this novel, Adam is said to be the physical size of an adult, but he does not work hard enough to be considered one, or at least, this is how Adam's father puts it. Adam is slow to finish his chores, and he continues to do childish things, such as reciting a superstitious chant over the family's drinking water. Moses, Adam's father, uses this as the measuring stick by which to judge whether Adam has indeed reached adulthood. By that measure, Adam has failed.

Topics for Further Study

- The names of towns and nearby villages are mentioned throughout *April Morning*. Create a map, either on paper or in a three dimensional medium such as papier-mâche´, of the countryside of Massachusetts as it was in 1775. Trace the progress of the British forces as they marched from Boston to Concord. Also map out the points at which the British met the colonists both on the way to Concord and on the way back to Boston. Match the details found in the novel with information you find in a reference book about the first encounters with the British on that day. Share your map with your class.

- Choose one of the characters in this

novel and draw a portrait of that person. The author provides a few clues as to how the characters might have looked, so use them as a guideline, but also research the type of clothing they might have worn to keep your sketches authentic with the times. Share the portrait with your class, allowing them to guess which character it might be before you tell them.

- Create a diary, writing as Ruth Simmons. Express her feelings for Adam Cooper before the confrontation with the British, while Adam was away fighting, and upon his return. Keep her character as written by the author in mind. Remember that she is a strong-willed young woman who has confessed her love for Adam. Also be mindful of the time she was living in. Otherwise, use your imagination in trying to guess what emotions she was having at critical moments in this story. Read the diary to your class.

- There are several Web sites that are used to promote modern towns and cities. Investigate a few of them to give you an idea of how they are set up and what information they provide. Then choose either Concord or Lexington and research the details of what these towns looked like and what they might have offered a visitor in colonial times (such as the early 1700s). Create a Web site using this information and photos from history books or online publications. Provide a brief history of the town and descriptions of the natural environment. Make up activities that you think tourists might have enjoyed back then, such as canoeing at a nearby river, hunting, or fishing. Where might visitors have gone to eat? What were the names of inns where they might have slept? Provide the Web address to your class and invite them to investigate your Web site.

- Read the young-adult novel *The Fighting Ground* by Avi Wortiz. Create a chart that compares and contrasts the experiences of Jonathan in *The Fighting Ground* with those of Adam, the protagonist in *April Morning*.

As the story progresses, though, Adam is thrown into the world of adult responsibilities. There, Adam faces the challenges and passes with honors into the adult world. He is praised by his father when he signs the muster book and commits himself to defending his village and standing up for the human rights his father has proposed. Later, Cousin Simmons and the Reverend praise Adam for his mature acceptance of his father's death and facing the hardships of war without complaining. When he returns home, Adam's mother leans on her son as if he had left the house a child but returned as a man.

Wars

A minor theme that runs through this novel is that of antiwar sentiment, set in the context of the American Revolutionary War. As the men in Lexington wait for the British Army to arrive, they argue about how they are going to confront the soldiers. Moses Cooper does not believe in war. He thinks that all conflicts should be solved through negotiation. Moses has a good mind for a logical argument and is used to winning the debates that he engages in. The Reverend, though he often likes to argue with Moses on other topics, agrees with Moses when it comes to the issue of war. He makes a strong stand against Solomon Chandler when Chandler suggests that God takes sides in a war. The Reverend believes that God is also against war and would take no one's side in a battle.

Adam also expresses his antiwar feelings. He is excited at first when he is allowed to sign the muster book. This makes him feel like a man.

However, after he sees the horrors that war can bring, Adam does not understand why anyone ever uses the excuse of a war to kill someone. It is through these characters and their expressions that the author makes his own antiwar sentiment apparent.

Freedom

There are two overarching themes of freedom or independence in this novel. The most obvious is the war that the colonists are willing to fight to rid their land of British dominance. The colonists have grown tired of paying the taxes that the British have imposed on them. They also want to make their own rules. They have come to the point where they believe they can stand on their own as a nation, so they want to make their declaration of freedom known. According to this novel, the majority of men in Lexington want to tell the British what they want. When the British do not listen, the colonists are willing to fight for their independence.

On another level, Adam, the protagonist, is also fighting for his freedom. He is tired of being looked upon as a child. He wants to be able to do what adults do. He wants to attend important meetings. He wants to do what he wants without limitations, whether this is to ship out with his uncle to the Indies or to court his neighbor, Ruth. When Adam finally wins his independence, though, it is met with some sadness. For example, he must say good-bye to his childhood. He also realizes that with his independence comes bigger responsibilities.

Style

Journal Writing

April Morning is written in a style that is similar to actual. It is as if the narrator, Adam, were keeping a diary. The style makes the reader feel like the story is being read while looking over Adam's shoulder as he records the details and events of his days. Adam either directly experiences what he records or he overhears someone else describe an event that he did not personally witness.

The shortcoming of a novel written in this way is that the reader receives only Adam's interpretations. The reader sees and feels what Adam sees and feels. No one knows how Ruth feels, for example, except through Adam's reactions to her. The same is true for all the other characters. Readers experience the story from the viewpoint of a male teenager. A female point of view is never provided, nor an adult interpretation. The strength of this journal type writing is that the author can go deep within the protagonist's mind, giving insight into Adam's emotions and his reflections. The war, for example, is described through Adam's fears as well as his lack of military prowess.

Historical Setting

By placing this fictional work in a historical

setting, the author accomplishes two things. First, he tells a story of a young eighteenth-century boy. Second, he also enhances the details of a historical event. Most readers might be familiar with the general context of the battles that took place in Lexington and Concord, but through this fictional account, readers are invited to share the incident on a personal level. It is as if one were there at the battle of Lexington, rather than merely reading historical data about the beginning of the Revolutionary War.

Much like the modern-day tactic of embedding reporters with a military troop in Iraq or Afghanistan so that people at home can read about the activities of the soldiers, this novel, set in the past, transports readers to the battlefield. In this way, readers can imagine what it might have been like to be involved in the colonists' fight for independence.

The Beginning of the Revolutionary War
The battle at Lexington, Massachusetts, as Fast recounts in his novel *April Morning*, was the first military conflict between the colonists and the British forces in 1775. This event would begin what was called the Revolutionary War, as the colonists fought for their independence from British rule. However, the tension between the British and the colonists started several years prior to this event.

In order to command control of the colonists and to make a profit, the British issued a series of taxes. They enforced taxes on sugar, printed materials, and paints. There was also a law that demanded that the colonists feed and house the British troops without compensation. In 1768, as tension rose, mostly in Boston, the governor of Massachusetts, Thomas Hutchinson, asked for and received an additional four thousand British soldiers to help preserve the peace. This action did not deter those who protested the British laws, and on March 5, 1770, a skirmish occurred in which five colonists were killed. This event was later referred to as the Boston Massacre; it increased the tensions between the colonists and the British forces.

In 1773, when the British Parliament passed a tax on tea, the colonists revolted by tossing a shipload of tea into the Boston Harbor. This came to be known at the Boston Tea Party. In retaliation, the

British closed Boston Harbor to all ship traffic. This meant that the colonists could not receive or ship out any goods. A year later, the colonists formed the First Continental Congress, during which time they appealed to the British king, George III, to repeal all the punishing acts. If the British did not respond favorably, the colonist stated that they were ready to refuse to buy all British goods sent to colonies.

It was under these conditions that fateful march took place, with the British Army moving toward Concord via Lexington. The British were aware that the colonists were agitated and had heard rumors that they might take some kind of rebellious military action, so when they learned that the colonists were storing supplies at Concord, the British decided to plan what they thought would be a covert maneuver. In the middle of the night, they set out from Boston, hoping the darkness would hide them. Their mission was to learn the truth of these rumors of stored goods and to destroy whatever they found.

There were reportedly between 640 and 900 British soldiers involved. They crossed the Charles River and were heading to Concord, less than twenty miles from Boston. In charge of the troops were Lt. Colonel Francis Smith and Major John Pitcairn. The British had witnessed very little military resistance by colonists up to this point and expected none to occur that day.

Compare & Contrast

- **1770s:** Colonial soldiers go to war with the British to gain their independence and to create the country of the United States of America.

  1960s: American soldiers go to war in Vietnam in an attempt to stop the communist takeover of South Vietnam.

  2000s: American soldiers go to war against terrorists who threaten their country's security.

- **1770s:** War is fought mostly on the ground with men face to face with their enemies, using rifles with attached bayonets.

  1960s: Bombs dropped from airplanes flying a thousand feet in the air destroy villages and kill masses of people without the pilots coming in contact with them.

  2000s: Destructive missiles can be launched from hundreds of miles away, with the soldiers never seeing their targeted victims.

- **1770s:** Messengers, such as Paul Revere, ride on horseback to deliver messages during the Revolutionary War.

  1960s: For the first time, images

from the battlefields are televised, sending coverage of the war from Vietnam to homes in the United States.

2000s: Soldiers can send messages via the Internet to families at home.

The colonists, in the meantime, organized by John Parker, waited in Lexington with guns in their hands. Upon arriving there, Pitcairn gave orders for his British troops to disarm the local militia. It was then that a shot rang out. To this day, no one is sure which side fired that first shot. Upon hearing the single gunshot, the British opened fired on the colonists, killing eight of the men and wounding ten others before the colonists retreated to the nearby woods. These actions thus became the first battle of many more to follow and would be later collectively known as the Revolutionary War.

The Minutemen

COMPARE & CONTRAST

Outside Boston, most of the adult male population of the surrounding areas of Massachusetts were farmers. Though they might also have been blacksmiths, furniture makers, and merchants, primarily the men worked the land to provide food for their families. In times of trouble, though, many of these men came to their town's call, with guns in hand, ready to protect their families and their economic interests. Out of this group of militia, a few men were chosen to become Minutemen. The name of this group of men reflected the fact that they were trained to be ready with only a minute's warning.

The Minutemen were often younger than the general population of the militia. They were around twenty-five years old and in good physical shape, and they were trained more vigorously than the older men. In 1775, the town of Concord was the first to create a group of Minutemen. It was the Minutemen of the surrounding area who met the British forces at North Bridge just outside Concord and gave the redcoats their first show of military opposition. Unfortunately, although the Minutemen were well trained, they lacked a unified leadership, so when various companies of Minutemen came together to fight the British, no one leader was in charge and confusion often reigned.

Critical Overview

In a tribute to Fast, written for *Booklist*, Brad Hooper states: "The bottom line is that when it comes to reading Howard Fast, we continue to understand and appreciate that simply, he could tell a darn good story." From reviews of Fast's books, whether written in the 1960s or twenty years later, most reviewers have the same sentiment. For historical novels, Fast is one of the best storytellers.

In 1961, when *April Morning* was first published, Kenneth Fearing reviewed it for the *New York Times*. Fearing writes that in this novel, "events move swiftly along in a nimbus of historic color and detail." He adds: "Howard Fast has admirably recaptured the sights and sound, the religious and political idioms, the simple military tactics and strategies of that day." In another review from the same time period, J. Donald Adams, also writing for the *New York Times*, states that *April Morning* was one of those rare books that he could not put down. "Another kind of book of the same length," Adams writes, "might well have taken me longer, but this was one of compelling narrative power, of unflagging interest."

In another tribute to Fast, Dennis McLellan, writing for the *Los Angeles Times*, calls Fast "one of the most widely read authors of the 20th century." In the *Guardian*, Eric Homberger refers to Fast as a "literary phenomenon" as well as a "champion of the progressive novel in the United States."

What Do I Read Next?

- Fast's fictionalized biography of the American Revolution, *Citizen Tom Paine* (1943), tells the story of the newly arrived patriot who woke the colonial citizenry with calls for "Common Sense." The novel weaves in the important figures of the revolutionary period while telling the story of Paine.

- James Lincoln Collier's *My Brother Sam Is Dead* (2005) tells the story of a family torn apart by the Revolutionary War, as the protagonist, Tim Meeker, must choose which side to fight on. In this young-adult novel, the author portrays both sides, the British and the revolutionaries, on equal terms as they wage war against each other. No matter which side Tim supports, he will end up fighting against one of his family members, his father or his older brother.

- In Ann Rinaldi's young-adult novel from 2004, *Cast Two Shadows: The American Revolution in the South*, the Revolutionary War is witnessed by fourteen-year-old Caroline Whitaker. The young teen loses her father when he refuses to support the British, and she watches as a friend is brutally murdered. Caroline also learns that her real mother is not the woman who has raised her but a former slave who used to work for the family. The mother and daughter are reunited as they share a mission to save Caroline's brother, who has been court-martialed.

- There is mention of slave ships in Fast's novel. The novel *Amistad* (1997), written by David Pesci and based on true events that occurred many years after the Revolution, is a fictional rendition of a real slave rebellion on one of those ships. The revolt occurred in 1839 and was ultimately unsuccessful. However, the incident brought the issue of slavery to the forefront of public debate.

- *Red, White, and Black: The Peoples of Early North America* (2005), written by Gary B. Nash, describes for readers the interconnectedness among Native Americans, African Americans, and European Americans during the colonial and revolutionary eras as they shared the land that would later become the United States.

- For a different look at early Americans about a hundred years after the Revolutionary War, Fast has written a series of books about immigrants. His first, *The Immigrant* (1977), follows a poor couple from Europe as they land in the United States and then travel from the East Coast to California looking for a new home and new life. Dan, their son, is born in a boxcar on a train and grows up determined to evade the poverty of his youth. The second book of the series, *Second Generation* (1978), is about Dan's daughter, Barbara, who grows up rejecting her father's wealth. The third novel is called *Establishment* (1979) and is set at the end of World War II. As Fast did in real life,

Barbara must face the House Un-American Activities Committee.

Sources

Adams, J. Donald, "Speaking of Books," in *New York Times*, May 14, 1961, p. BR2.

Fast, Howard, *April Morning*, Bantam Books, 1961.

Fearing, Kenneth, "A Meeting at Concord," in *New York Times*, April 23, 1961, p. 438.

Griffith, Samuel B., "An Affair That Happened on the Nineteenth Inst.," in *The War for American Independence: From 1760 to the Surrender at Yorktown in 1781*, University of Illinois Press, 2002, pp. 157–74.

Homberger, Eric, "Howard Fast: Prolific Radical Novelist Who Championed the Cause of America's Common People," in *Guardian* (London, England), March 14, 2003, p. 25.

Hooper, Brad, "A Tribute to Howard Fast," in *Booklist*, May 15, 2003, Vol. 99, No. 18, p. 1639.

McLellan, Dennis, "Howard Fast, 88; Novels Included *Spartacus*," in *Los Angeles Times*, March 14, 2003, p. B.13.

"Sowing the Seeds of Liberty: Lexington and the American Revolution," in *National Heritage Museum*, http://www.nationalheritagemuseum.org/Default.asp tabid= 162 (accessed December 18, 2009).

"Today in History: April 19," in *Library of Congress: American Memory*,

http://memory.loc.gov/ammem/today/apr19.html
(accessed December 16, 2009).

Further Reading

Emerson, Ralph Waldo, *The Complete Works of Ralph Waldo Emerson*, General Books, 2009.

> Emerson, whose grandfather was involved in the first battles of the Revolutionary War, wrote a poem in honor of the men who lost their lives fighting the British in the 1700s. It is from Emerson's "Concord Hymn" that the famous line about the first shot fired in Lexington being heard around the world is taken.

Ferling, John, *Almost a Miracle: The American Victory in the War of Independence*, Oxford University Press, 2009.

> This concise history of the Revolutionary War, written by a distinguished historian whose research is notably extensive, is well worth the effort of reading. This book offers the story of the endurance of the colonists, which caught the British off guard and eventually helped the colonists to win their independence.

Fischer, David Hackett, *Paul Revere's Ride*, Oxford University Press, 1995.

> This young-adult book provides an

extensive story about the young messenger who rode his horse ahead of the British forces to warn the colonists of their coming. Though Fast does not name the messenger in his novel, Paul Revere is the figure most often referred to as the one who rode through the night so the colonists would not be unprepared. Though he was a somewhat minor character in the war, Paul Revere's ride was a pivotal event that helped the colonists gain victory.

Galvin, John R., *The Minute Men: The First Fight: Myths and Realities of the American Revolution*, Potomac Books, 2006.

The Minutemen were an intricate part of the Revolutionary War, and this book explains who they were. As the author sorts through the stories, disclaiming some of the myths and supporting the facts, readers learn about the lives of these ordinary farmers and shopkeepers who quickly transformed themselves into soldiers when they were needed.

Scheer, George, and Hugh F. Rankin, *Rebels and Redcoats: The American Revolution through the Eyes of Those That Fought and Lived It*, DaCapo Press, 1987.

Written in a narrative style with

comments from people who lived through it, this tale of the American Revolution is told through the experiences of both the colonists and the British soldiers who were on the battlefield. Research was done on the major players of this great battle for independence, such as George Washington and Benjamin Franklin, but the authors also capture how the foot soldiers endured this war.

Tourtellot, Arthur Bernon, *Lexington and Concord: The Beginning of the War of the American Revolution*, W. W. Norton, 2000.

Here are the historical facts of the first days of the Revolutionary War as presented in Fast's novel. Tourtellot describes the roles that two Massachusetts towns, Lexington and Concord, played in starting the colonists' fight for freedom.

Suggested Search Terms

Howard Fast bio Howard Fast

AND April Morning

Howard Fast novels

April Morning AND young adult novel

April Morning AND Revolutionary War

April Morning AND American Revolution

April Morning AND Lexington and Concord

April Morning AND minutemen

April Morning AND bildungsroman

CPSIA information can be obtained
at www.ICGtesting.com
Printed in the USA
BVHW091327260819
556817BV00015B/1759/P

9 781375 376396